AF480797

The Final Screen Play:

The King of Faust

OMNI

ISBN:979-8-3492-1671-8

DEDICATION

For every soul who's been silenced, erased, or overlooked.

For the ones who lost faith, then found it again.

For the children growing in the shadow of our decisions.

May we do better.

And may they write a brighter final scene

Then we could ever imagine.

CONTENTS

| | Acknowledgments | i |
| Prologue | The Devil's Bargain | Pg 1 |

ACT I — The Summons

Scene I	Smoke and Mirrors	Pg 5
Scene II	The Apprentice Curse	Pg 7
Scene III	A Nation for Sale	Pg 9
Scene IV	The Echo Chamber	Pg 11
Scene V	The Enemy Within	Pg 14
Scene VI	The Bargain	Pg 17
Scene VII	The Anointed	Pg 20

ACT II — Cult of Personality

Scene I	The Transformation	Pg 25
Scene II	The Engine that Feeds	Pg 28
Scene III	How Belief is Structured	Pg 33
Scene IV	The Architects	Pg 36
Scene V	Myth-Fixation Response	Pg 39
Scene VI	The Mirror Cracking	Pg 43
Scene VII	The Theater of Obedience	Pg 47
Scene VIII	The Machinery of Fear	Pg 50

Scene IX   Disappearance of Dignity   Pg 53

Scene X   The Unseen Puppet Master   Pg 56

ACT III   The Reckoning

Scene I   The Gathering Storm   Pg 59

Scene II   The Wreckage   Pg 61

Scene III   The Moment   Pg 64

Scene IV   The Awakening   Pg 67

Scene V   The Reckoning   Pg 69

Scene VI   The Rebuild   Pg 72

Scene VII   The Lesson   Pg 75

Scene VIII   The Final Curtain   Pg 78

ACKNOWLEDGMENTS

To those who never looked away.

To the whistleblowers, the truth-tellers,

The quiet resisters who held the line when

The noise grew deafening.

To the journalists who kept digging.

To the historians who reminded us that

We've seen this before.

To the teachers who planted seeds of

Critical thought.

To the artists who turned outrage into beauty.

To the everyday people who refused to be numb.

To the law enforcement officers who

Served with honor and integrity and to

Those who made the ultimate sacrifice in

The line of duty.

To those who stood firm in the light of

Truth, even when it meant standing alone.

To my family and friends, whose

Unwavering support and belief in this

Journey has been my anchor.

Your love and encouragement have been the

Bedrock upon which this work stands.

PROLOGUE: THE DEVIL'S BARGAIN

It begins with a mirror. Once whole. Now shattered. The fragments reflect not only a face but the fractured soul of a nation. This is the FAUST – warped by delusion, cracked by ambition, crowned by hubris.

A crown rests atop the broken glass – unshaken, unearned. Not placed there by grace, but seized by those who mistake chaos for strength.

This is no ordinary tale. It is a final screenplay. And we are all in it, whether we admit it or not.

There comes a moment in every nation's story when a deal is made.

Not with gold or land.

Not even with blood.

But with the soul.

It begins with a whisper.

A voice that doesn't shout – it insinuates.

A smirk behind a podium.

A finger pointed at "them," not "us."

A crowd stirred, not by truth, but by spectacle.

He promised power.

He promised restoration.

He promised that only He could *fix* it.

And the people listened – not all, but enough.

They traded discomfort for delusion.

Morality for momentum.

Integrity for identity.

This star does not wear a crown.

He wears ego, arrogance, and a smirk that says, "I can do anything.

And they will cheer anyway."

This is not fiction.

It is the slow erosion of conscience.

The rise of a cult built not on principle but on personality.

A nation's compass, once fixed on justice, now spins wildly towards whatever feels good, whatever seems strong, whatever has promised to win.

The curtain has not yet fallen.

There is time still.

But not forever.

Mephistopheles collecting a soul. Created by Chat GPT

Introduction

The Legend of Faust

There is a legend, long buried beneath the dust of time, nearly forgotten now.

Passed from mouth to mouth, reshaped by fear and fascination, it has slipped through the cracks of history like smoke through old stone. It tells of a man who bartered his soul not for love or justice, but for power, unrestrained and absolute. His name still lingers, though the truth of his descent has been lost in the telling. But every era has its Faust. Every age finds a man willing to trade the sacred for the self.

A man named Faust – brilliant, restless, and insatiable – grew weary of the limitations of human knowledge. He wanted more. More power, more influence, more pleasure. And soon he struck a deal with Mephistopheles, the clever emissary of darkness. The bargain was simple: Faust would gain everything he desired in exchange for his soul.

At first, the world bent to his will. He was adored, feared, and followed. Slowly, the cost revealed itself, not in fire or brimstone, but in the erosion of truth, decency, and human dignity. Ultimately, it was not the devil with horns who destroyed Faust; it was Faust himself.

This is not just a tale of one man. It is the tale of all who believe they can outwit Consequence. It is the story of what happens when ego replaces empathy, and ambition erases morality. Mephistopheles does not appear in a puff of smoke. He arrives in applause, wrapped in promises, disguised as destiny.

This is not fiction.

It is a mirror.

A mirror cracked.

ACT I: The Summons

Scene I: Smoke and Mirrors

There was no thunderclap.

No rending of the heavens.

Just spectacle. A glow of studio lights.

A descending escalator.

And a man – Him - waving like a messiah stepping onto center stage.

Not elected yet, but already worshipped.

He came not to lead, but to seduce.

Not with policy, but with performance.

Not with clarity, but with chaos.

He didn't need truth.

He only needed doubt.

Doubt is fertile ground for tyranny.

He insulted, mocked, belittled, and dominated.

A master of television turned messiah to the disillusioned.

They had watched Him fire people for ratings.

Now they begged Him to fire up a nation.

He offered them a villain for every ill:

Immigrants.

Journalists.

Scientists.

Truth itself.

And they followed.

Not because He was good.

But because He was entertaining.

Because He made them feel powerful.

By giving them someone to blame.

Meanwhile, the foundations shook.

Laws bent to His wants.

Language warped until cruelty seemed courageous.

And corruption sounded like strength.

The circus had come to town,

And the ringmaster wore a red cap.

Scene II: The Apprentice's Curse

Before He was crowned by ballot and blind loyalty,

He was schooled by a different kind of power.

A man named Roy

Whose name history now speaks with a wince.

Roy taught Him that truth was weakness.

That decency was a liability.

And that shame was optional.

Never apologize. Never admit fault. Attack, sue, destroy.

The lessons were carved into His marrow.

Like commandments.

It wasn't politics He learned. It was war.

A cold, smiling war.

Fought with lawsuits, lies, and limitless ego.

And, so he practiced.

On business rivals.

On banks.

On the media.

On anyone who dared to question the myth of *Him*.

Roy, the ghost of McCarthyism,

passed Him the torch of fear-mongering

And spectacle.

And He ran with it.

Torching every bridge to reason in His path.

He became not a servant of democracy

But a salesman of delusion.

Each failure was someone else's fault.

Each victory was divine confirmation of

His greatness.

This was no leader–in–waiting.

This was the **King of Faust.**

Signing the contract in invisible ink.

The price would be due later.

It always is.

Scene III: A Nation for Sale

It began with applause.

With hats.

With slogans carved in nostalgia and fear.

He didn't promise unity. He promised a return.

To a myth that never was.

He did not rise to lead the people.

He rose because they wanted someone to speak their rage aloud.

And He did.

Over and over, He did.

He did not build coalitions.

He built cults.

And sold His name like a sacred brand.

From hotels to steaks to hats to hope.

Truth became malleable.

Shaped by tweets and tantrums.

What mattered was not what was real,

But what was believed.

He did not sell policy.

He sold personality.

The personality of power—

raw, unapologetic, and cruel.

And the nation bought it.

Bought Him.

Bought the circus.

Not with money.

But with integrity.

With decency.

With the blood of truth itself.

Democracy was not stolen.

It was pawned.

And no one read the fine print.

Scene IV: The Echo Chamber

Truth used to stand alone.

Now it shouts into a mirror.

And hears only its own distortion.

He did not need to silence the press.

He only needed to discredit it.

"Fake news," He chanted.

And suddenly, facts were optional.

He poisoned the well of knowledge.

One drop at a time.

Soon, every credible voice was suspect.

Scientists.

Historians.

Judges.

Anyone who contradicted His narrative

Was labeled a traitor.

He created His own reality.

And forced a nation to live in it.

The media that praised Him was real.

Everything else was a lie, fake.

Not wrong -- *evil.*

It was not ignorance He cultivated,

but loyalty stronger than evidence.

He built a *fortress of delusion --*

A glittering palace of mirrors,

Each reflection showing only His face.

With walls made of algorithms.

And gates kept by outrage.

Once inside,

Truth had no voice --

Only echo.

Education became elitist.

Expertise became suspect.

Critical thought became treasonous.

He did not conquer by force.

He conquered by repetition.

The people stopped asking questions.

And the silence was deafening.

Scene V: The Enemy Within

He didn't need foreign armies.

He found His soldiers at home.

Not in uniform, but in red hats with gold letters.

Carrying flags they barely understood.

He didn't point outward.

He pointed inward.

Neighbors became suspects.

Friends became foes.

Truth became a matter of allegiance.

The enemy, He claimed,

was already here.

In the schools.

In the cities.

In the voting booths.

He turned citizen against citizen.

He weaponized patriotism.

Made it a blade

Sharpened against the other.

Suddenly, protest was sedition.

Dissent was treason.

Justice, a witch hunt.

The institutions meant to hold Him back

Became His battlegrounds.

Courts were corrupted.

Legislators cowered.

Law became theater.

And while they argued over decorum,

He redefined power.

Not as governance,

But as domination.

He had no need for facts.

Only fear and doubt.

And fear was in abundance.

Not imported.

Not foreign.

Homegrown.

The enemy had no accent.

The enemy bore no flag.

The enemy looked like us.

Because it was us.

Scene VI: The Bargain

He never made promises.

He made deals.

He dangled illusions

Like jewels before a restless crowd.

Each one reflecting what they most longed to see.

He knew what they wanted.

To feel seen.

To feel heard.

To feel *right*.

And He offered it all.

Security, prosperity, greatness.

But not for free.

They didn't realize

they were signing a contract.

Not in ink.

In silence.

In complicity.

The price wasn't money.

It was conscience.

They gave up kindness

For a glimpse of power.

They surrendered truth

for the thrill of being on the winning team.

They thought they could walk away

Once the deal soured.

But Faust never walks away clean.

And neither did they.

They stood by as He punished the

Innocent,

Rewrote the rules,

And mocked the weak.

But they didn't just stand by.

They Cheered.

They Cheered when he imitated a man

With a disability.

Laughed as he contorted his body into

Cruelty.

It was broadcast again and again.

A stain played like a spectacle.

And still –

They cheered.

They stood by,

telling themselves it was just noise.

But it wasn't noise.

It was the sound of the floor falling out

beneath them.

They did not sell their souls in a moment.

They lost them

One excuse at a time.

Scene VII: The Anointed

They held the Book upside down.

They stood beside Him, smiling.

They called him chosen.

Not because he healed.

But because he conquered.

They did not recognize the wolf –

The predator disguised as protector.

Or perhaps they did.

And chose to follow;

Believing his darkness would shield them.

He did not speak of grace.

He boasted.

He bullied.

He lied.

And they nodded.

They traded the Sermon on the Mount

For a Throne on Earth.

Traded love for loyalty.

Traded humility for might.

He mocked the broken.

They blessed him.

He sowed division.

They laid hands on Him.

He built a golden tower.

They called it holy ground.

He did not come in peace.

He came with spectacle and scorn.

He did not turn over the tables.

He sat at them.

Surrounded by those who once claimed to

Follow Christ.

He offered no parables.

Only promises.

No wisdom.

Only walls.

And they rejoiced.

They called him strong.

They called him protector.

They called him theirs.

They did not ask what spirit filled the

Room.

They only asked:

"Will he fight for us?"

And when he cursed the stranger --

They cheered.

When he mocked the sick --

They laughed.

When he twisted truth –

They quoted him like scripture.

They forgot that love is patient.

That love is kind.

That love does not envy,

Does not boast,

Is not proud.

They forgot the poor.

They forgot the meek.

They forgot the peacemakers.

They forgot themselves.

They were meant to help us protect our souls.

To be moral compasses.

Moral authorities.

Voices of truth in a world of noise.

Instead, our souls were lost.

Not in fire.

But in silence.

In justification.

In applause.

We became immune to guilt.

Numb to shame.

Pride disguised as righteousness.

This was not worship.

It was a trade.

A kingdom not of heaven –

But of *fear.*

And still, they bowed.

Not to God.

But to a man who promised them power

In exchange for their silence.

ACT II: Cult of Personality

Scene I: The Transformation

It doesn't happen all at once.

The transformation is **slow**.

It begins not with belief.

But with **confusion.**

Facts are bent just slightly.

Not enough to be questioned.

Just enough to be doubted.

Certainty begins to feel naïve.

People don't stop trusting truth overnight.

They begin to wonder if anyone is telling

The truth.

If maybe no one knows.

And in that uncertainty –

A new voice rises.

One that sounds confident.

One that sounds simple.

One that demands nothing

But agreement.

This is how a story is rewritten.

Trusted sources are cast as corrupt.

Questions are reframed as attacks.

Contradiction floods the senses.

Until only one message remains.

Loud enough

To feel like clarity.

And then – **REPETITION, repetition, repetition, repetition**

Not information.

Not discussion.

Just repetition.

Say it loud enough.

Say it often enough.

Say it without shame.

And it begins to feel true.

This is not education.

It is **emotional conditioning.**

What once felt shocking becomes

Routine.

What once felt offensive becomes

Amusing.

What once felt

Impossible

Becomes inevitable.

This is not the opening of the mind.

It is the narrowing of thought.

Wrapped in the illusion of certainty,

And sealed by the comfort of belonging.

In that warmth,

Truth became negotiable.

And obedience was mistaken

For virtue.

Scene II: The Engine That Feeds

It does not sleep.

It does not think.

It does not judge.

It only feeds.

Not on truth.

But on **attention.**

Every click is a signal.

Every like, a breadcrumb.

Every pause, a whisper:

More of this.

This is not **coincidence.**

It is **design.**

The engine doesn't care what you believe.

It only cares that you stay.

So, it watches –

How long you linger.

What makes you angry.

What makes you scared.

Then it builds a world around you.

Not a world of facts –

But a world of **_confirmation_**.

This is **information bias** on autopilot.

A reality shaped not by knowledge,

But by *desire*.

And the longer you stay,

The narrower **your world becomes**.

Voices disappear.

Contradictions vanish.

Complexity fades.

Until there is only one truth –

Yours.

And **if you see it everywhere,**

It must be real.

Right?

It doesn't stop at content.

It moves deeper.

Into **behavior**.

Into **emotion**.

Into the intimate data of your daily life.

The engine learns what frightens you.

What enrages you.

What gives you a fleeting sense of

Purpose.

And it uses that --

To keep **you scrolling**.

To keep you inside.

To keep you fed.

You were not just watching the story.

You were being written into it.

Artificial **intelligence maps the** soul.

Not with understanding,

But with prediction.

It doesn't know you.

It doesn't need to.

It only knows how to sort you -

Into patterns,

Into pathways,

Into *piles of probability*.

Are you anxious?

Here's fear.

Are you lonely?

Here's outrage.

Are you insecure?

Here's someone to blame.

Are you isolated?

Here's purpose -- wrapped in the warmth

Of community.

Even if the fire was false.

This is not just media.

This is a **mirror** –

Curated to your bias.

Reflected through an algorithm

That knows you better

Then you know yourself.

And behind the **curtain**,

Someone is watching the numbers.

Testing the messages.

Weaponizing belief.

To shape elections.

To seed division.

To monetize rage.

You are not the audience.

You are the product.

And the engine that feeds

Never stops feeding.

Scene III: How Belief is Structured (emotional and
psychological anatomy of belief)

Belief is not born.

It is **built.**

It begins with a whisper –

A headline.

A post.

A glance that feels true.

Before it's ever questioned.

Not because it is true.

But because it is familiar.

Familiarity breeds comfort.

Comfort breeds trust.

And trust, once given,

Rarely asks for proof.

This is the first layer.

Then comes **emotion.**

Fear.

Anger.

Pride.

Shame.

Emotion seals the message.

Makes it stick.

Because we don't protect facts.

We protect feelings

About facts.

The next layer is **Identity.**

If I believe this,

Then this is who I am.

If I stop believing,

Who am I now?

Belief becomes armor.

It becomes tribe.

It becomes home.

And once belief becomes identity --

Truth is no longer the goal.

Only **confirmation.**

And with each echo,

The self hardens.

Doubt becomes betrayal.

And Dialogue dies.

Scene IV: The Architects

Belief doesn't need to be true.

It only needs to be **useful.**

And those who understand that --

The architects --

Use it not to enlighten,

But to control.

They do not deal in facts.

They deal in *feelings disguised as*

Certainty.

They know how belief is structured.

They know the mind will protect what it

Needs to feel safe.

Even if it's false.

So, they build the message accordingly:

Fear.

Blame.

Belonging.

A villain.

A savior.

A war to win.

They don't care what people believe.

Only *why* they believe.

And once that need is known,

Everything can be shaped.

With algorithms.

With data.

With outrage.

They create a reality that feels inevitable –

Because it feels **personal.**

It doesn't have to be real.

It only has to be repeated.

Framed.

Reinforced.

Rewarded.

And over time,

What begins as opinion

Becomes identity.

This is the work of *The Architects*.

Not tyrants in uniform.

But marketers in boardrooms.

Coders behind curtains.

Data engines pulling information,

Assembling the architecture of belief.

An invisible machine tuned to the frequency of desire.

They are not merely building belief.

They're engineering conviction.

Unyielding, unquestioned,

And designed to endure.

Scene V: Myth-Fixation Response

There comes a point

When belief is no longer about truth.

It becomes about meaning.

And once a belief gives someone

Meaning,

It becomes untouchable.

Even if the facts collapse.

Even if the story breaks.

Even if the hero fails.

This is called the *Myth-Fixation Response.*

It is the psychological reflex

To protect the myth

That gives us identity –

Even at the expense of reality.

It doesn't happen out of ignorance.

It happens out of need.

Because if the myth is false,

What does that make us?

If the man we believed in is a fraud,

What does that say about our judgment?

Our tribe?

Our soul?

It's easier to fight the facts

Then to face that kind of grief.

So, the mind builds defenses.

Every contradiction is an attack.

Every critic is a traitor.

Every question is an insult.

And the myth becomes sacred.

Not because it is pure,

But because it is ours.

And when the myth is threatened —

The response isn't retreat.

It's **doubling down.**

Not because the believer is blind.

But because they are *bound.*

To abandon the belief

Would mean unraveling the self.

So, the mind fortifies.

It rejects new information.

It reframes contradiction as persecution.

Builds walls out of loyalty,

And paints them with pride.

This is not stupidity.

It is **psychological survival.**

When truth threatens meaning,

Meaning wins.

It has to win when our inner

Peace is under attack.

This is the core of the

Myth-Fixation Response:

The soul choosing safety

Over self-awareness.

Identity choosing preservation

Over transformation.

And so, the lie lives on -

Not because it is strong,

But because *letting it die*

Would feel like dying with it.

Scene VI: The Mirror Cracking (Explores the fragmentation
of movements, shifting Consensus Reality, and the implosion of unity)

Every movement begins with a mirror.

A reflection of hope, anger, fear –

Shared by many,

Believed by more.

But over time,

The mirror begins to crack.

Not because of outside force,

But from the pressure within.

The myth demands purity.

The message demands loyalty.

The identity demands agreement.

And when disagreement appears –

Even slightly --

It becomes betrayal.

So, the movement tightens.

Narrows.

Sharpens.

Until those who once stood shoulder to shoulder

Become threats to each other's beliefs.

What began as unity

Fractures into factions.

Each group convinced they hold the

Truest version

Of the cause.

There is no single reality.

Only consensus reality.

A shared belief in what is true.

What is right.

What is real.

But consensus is fragile.

It doesn't live in facts.

It lives in agreement.

And agreement depends on trust,

On shared experience,

On the feeling that we see the same world.

But when a movement fractures,

So does its reality.

Each splinter sees itself as whole.

Each claims to be the original reflection.

Each reshapes the narrative

To match its own wound,

Its own fear,

Its own history.

Reality is no longer stable.

It becomes relational.

Shifting.

Personal.

Conditional.

What is true for one

Is false for another.

Not because of logic,

But because of lived experience.

Truth becomes a mirror,

Cracked in many directions.

Each shard sharp,

Each angle distorted,

Each piece claims to be the center.

46

And in that chaos,

The original purpose is lost.

The cause devours itself.

Scene VII: The Theater of Obedience

He understood the stage.

Not as a place for truth --

But for spectacle.

He didn't govern.

He performed.

Every rally, a sermon.

Every outburst, a script.

The crowd wasn't listening for answers.

They were listening for cues.

Applause.

Laughter.

Chants.

It didn't matter what He said.

Only that He said it with fire.

Obedience didn't come from force.

It came from rhythm.

Repetition.

Rehearsed outrage.

He gave them enemies to boo.

Heroes to cheer.

And Himself --

A martyr, a savior,

A misunderstood king.

The press became hecklers.

Science, a side act.

The law, a prop.

And the audience,

Hungry for certainty,

Became part of the play.

They wore the costumes.

Spoke the lines.

Silenced those who forgot their role.

This was no town hall.

This was a coliseum.

And He-

The showman of grievance --

Knew how to keep the crowd coming

Back.

Not with policy.

Not with progress.

But with drama.

Scene VIII: The Machinery of Fear

Fear was His currency.

Fear was His foundation.

Fear was the thing He traded in every deal.

It didn't have to be real.

It just had to be felt.

He painted threats on every corner.

Whispers of enemies at the gates.

Dangers unseen.

Monsters lurking in the shadows.

He didn't need to prove the threats.

He just needed to remind them that they

Might be real.

He didn't need to offer protection.

He just needed to be the only one claiming it.

And they believed Him.

Not because He was honest.

But because He knows how to make them

Scared enough to trust anyone

Who promised a sliver of safety.

The economy crumbled under

Uncertainty.

But they didn't see it as a failure.

They saw it as a call to arms.

A justification for the chaos He stirred,

The urgency He manufactured.

The news outlets, once trusted,

Became adversaries,

Spreading lies,

Distorting facts.

The truth was irrelevant.

Only His version of reality mattered.

He made them question their neighbors.

He made them suspicious of the

Unfamiliar.

He made them afraid of themselves.

Afraid of everything but Him.

And with that fear,

He built His empire.

Scene IX: The Disappearance of Dignity

Dignity became a casualty in the theater

Of His Rule.

It wasn't lost in a single moment.

It wasn't stolen by force.

It simply evaporated.

Slowly.

Imperceptibly.

Until one day, no one remembered its

Name.

He mocked it.

He belittled it.

He degraded it.

And the world watched.

Not in outrage,

But in disbelief.

The press, once a check on power,

Became complicit in the spectacle.

The people, once a voice of reason,

Became a chorus of hollow approval.

He didn't seek to lead with wisdom and morality.

He led with twisted and distorted facts.

He led with threats dressed as warnings.

And innuendo whispered into the

Ears of the uncertain.

He traded respect for reverence,

And dignity for devotion.

He didn't build trust.

He demanded loyalty.

In the process,

The people learned to bend.

To lower their eyes, turn their heads,

And excuse what had once been

Unthinkable.

No one spoke out.

At least, no one who mattered.

The noise of dissent was drowned out by

The roar of acceptance,

The hum of compliance.

And dignity?

It became a relic.

Dismissed, discarded, as hollow

As the promises He made.

Scene X: The Unseen Puppet Master

Behind every move,

Behind every word,

There was always a hand,

Invisible,

Pulling the strings.

The public saw only what He wanted them

To see.

The show,

The spectacle,

The persona.

But behind the curtain,

In the shadows,

The real power moved.

A whisper here,

A suggestion there,

Subtle nudges toward the outcome He

Desired.

The media, the politicians,

The people --

All were puppets,

Willing or otherwise,

Dancing to a tune they didn't know

Was being played.

He didn't need to shout commands.

He only needed to plant seeds of doubt.

He didn't need to force a direction.

He only needed to pull the right strings at

The right time.

He had mastered the **Art of Mass Manipulation**,

Not through force,

But with Finesse.

Through suggestion.

And the careful orchestration of

Chaos.

A move here,

A tweet there,

And the world spun.

Spun in His direction.

It was brilliance.

It was deceit.

It was terrifying.

And no one knew who was pulling them.

ACT III: The Reckoning

Scene I: The Gathering Storm

The winds had already started to shift,

But no one noticed until the storm had arrived.

He had sown the seeds of division.

And now, the clouds began to form.

The fissures in society deepened.

Torn apart by hate, greed, and fear.

The cries of the voiceless

Were drowned out by the thundering

Rhetoric of division.

The innocent were caught in the crossfire.

Blamed and silenced.

As the thunder roared louder.

The storm He had unleashed didn't care

Who it consumed.

It didn't care who it destroyed.

It only cared that the chaos grew.

Those who had followed Him blindly

Were now swept up in the torrents.

Lost in a deluge of fake news,

Manipulated truths, and fractured realities.

But the storm didn't end there.

It grew in intensity,

Gathering power from every whisper of

Hate,

Every betrayal of decency.

It became His creation.

Something He could wield.

A force He could control.

And as the clouds grew darker,

He stood at the center,

The eye of the storm.

The chaos was His to command,

And He reveled in it

Scene II: The Wreckage

All storms eventually lose their strength,

But the damage they leave behind can last

Forever.

The winds had calmed,

But the wreckage was everywhere.

The shattered pieces of truth,

The broken lives of those who had been

Swept up,

Were now left to pick up the pieces.

The reckoning had arrived.

It wasn't loud or violent,

It was quiet,

Sneaky,

Slowly seeping into the hearts and minds of those who had been

Blinded by His

Power.

The truth always catches up.

It had always been there,

Just beneath the surface,

Waiting to be uncovered.

And now, the reality of what had been

Allowed to happen began to sink in.

The empire He had built was crumbling.

The lies that had held it together

Were unraveling thread by thread.

People began to see the truth.

The truth they had ignored for so long.

The truth they had allowed to slip through

Their fingers.

The reckoning wasn't about punishment.

It wasn't about revenge.

It was about waking up,

About facing what had been done,

And understanding the cost of it all.

It wasn't too late to change.

It wasn't too late to rebuild.

But first, the truth had to be

Acknowledged.

The storm had passed.

But the real challenge was just beginning.

And it was up to the people to decide whether they would rebuild

Or repeat the cycle.

Scene III: The Moment

Every generation is offered a moment --

A chance to define who they are,

What they stand for,

And what they refuse to allow ever again.

This was that moment.

Standing at the crossroads of history,

The people faced a decision

That would ripple into generations not yet

Born.

They could look away.

Pretend it never happened.

Bury the evidence.

Rewrite the books.

Sanitize the truth.

Or they could face it.

Stand in it.

Own it.

And grow from it.

The Choice is not between Left or Right,

Not between Red or Blue.

It was deeper.

It was moral.

It was spiritual.

It was about character.

To choose accountability over comfort.

To choose truth over tribalism.

To choose growth over fear.

To choose the hard thing because it is

The right thing.

A nation that had once prided itself on its

Ideals

Had to decide whether it would be true to them,

Or let them erode beneath the

Convenience of Denial.

The script is still being written.

The ending has not been determined.

But the pen…

Is now in the hands of the people.

Scene IV: The Awakening

It began quietly.

Not with a roar,

But a murmur.

Whispers in classrooms.

Questions in churches.

Sideways glances exchanged in grocery

Stores.

The sense that something was not right.

The Awakening was not a revolution of

Violence.

It was a remembering.

Of values buried under slogans.

Of decency once taught at dinner tables.

Of compassion that had been dismissed

As weakness.

It came in unlikely places --

In the eyes of a child,

Seeing clearly what the

World refused to name.

In the quiet courage of a teacher who
Refused to rewrite the past.
In the stubborn kindness of a nurse who
Cared for the forgotten.

One by one,
They began to rise.
Not in rage,
But in resolve.

A consciousness stirred.
Not a political one.
A human one.

And with it came the realization:
We are not spectators in this story.
We are the authors of what comes next.

Scene V: The Reckoning

The tide does not apologize when it

Returns.

It simply arrives,

Carrying with it all that was cast out to sea.

This was not vengeance.

It was accounting.

For every truth bent beyond recognition.

For every voice silenced under the weight

Of mockery.

For every sacred trust sold for applause.

And every law reshaped to serve only one.

The Reckoning came

Not from above

But from below --

From the people who had watched in horror,

Frozen by disbelief,

Numb from the noise.

They had been told their outrage was

Overreaction.

That what they saw with their eyes

Was not real.

But clarity, once found, does not fade.

What was once unthinkable

Had become normalized.

Cruelty had become policy.

And lies had become the oxygen we breathe.

The Absurd was believed.

And still-

Truth had a pulse,

It beats beneath the surface.

Waiting for hearts and minds to tune in.

Laws once twisted began to realign.

Those who hid behind the veil of power

Were dragged into the light,

Where excuses dissolve

And actions stand alone.

It was not swift.

It was not clean.

But it was **Just**.

Because the soul of a nation --

Though bruised, though weary --

Remembers how to heal.

And healing always begins

With telling the truth.

Not just the truth of facts,

But the deeper truth,

The kind that lives beneath the noise,

That echoes in the soul before it's

Spoken.

The truth that aligns us with something

Eternal --

Older than nations, stronger than fear,

And untouched by power or pride.

Scene VI: The Rebuild

It began not with fireworks,

But with silence.

A hush across the land,

As if the nation itself exhaled

After holding its breath for too long.

The lights came back on in the places

Truth had been dimmed.

The books were opened.

The classrooms filled.

The conversations were hard, but real.

No one pretended it hadn't happened.

They etched it into history

So it could never happen again.

Statues were removed --

Not to erase,

But to acknowledge.

Children asked hard questions.
And this time,
The adults answered them.

The rebuild was not about bricks and marble,
But conscience and courage.

It was neighbors speaking to neighbors.
It was facts reclaiming the headlines.
It was art that dared to reflect the pain,
And the hope.

And in the center of it all,
A battered compass,
Still pointing true north.

Because after Faust,
After the deal,
After the fire --

Came the reckoning.
And after the reckoning,
Came the rebuild.

The people rose.

Not to follow.

But to lead.

Scene VII: The Lesson

Every era leaves a scar.

This one was carved deep.

But scars are stories --

Not just of the wound,

But of the healing.

The lesson was never about Him.

It was about Us.

How easily we gave it away:

Our voice.

Our vigilance.

Our virtue.

How quickly we accepted a lie when it

Was wrapped in a flag.

How silence masqueraded as peace.

How comfort became complicity.

Faust was not evil.

He was human.

Tempted.

Impatient.

Hungry.

Just like us.

But the true tragedy was not the deal --
It was forgetting the price.

The lesson is not just for now.
It is for the next time
And the time after that.

To remember that truth is fragile,
But not weak.
That conscience must be louder than
Charisma.
That power without humility
Is always a mask for something darker.

The lesson is not about fear.
It's about memory.

So we do not repeat.

So we do not forget.

Scene VIII: The Final Curtain

The lights dim.

Not because the show has ended,

But because the audience must now

Decide what comes next.

He fades into the wings,

But his shadow remains --

Etched into law,

Carved into culture,

Whispered in the halls of a

Fractured nation.

Applause fades into questions.

Cheers dissolve into consequences.

The stage is ours now.

Will we rewrite the script?

Or wait for another Him to rise,

With simpler lies and louder applause?

There are no second takes.

No edits.

No chance to rewrite the scene once

It's played.

The final curtain only falls

When we stop watching

Stop listening.

Stop caring.

But not yet.

Because the actors are still on stage --

Us.

Because the next line has yet to be written.

And redemption was never about the fall --

It has always lived in the rising.

The next act belongs to us.

Epilogue: The Mirror

History does not repeat itself.

It waits.

Patiently.

Quietly.

Until we forget.

And then it whispers.

Not as prophecy,

But as consequence.

He was never the beginning.

He was the reflection.

A mirror held up to a country too

Distracted to look.

Too entertained to care.

Too divided to unite.

He promised greatness,

But sold grievance.

He offered truth,

But delivered performance.

He labeled dissent as treason,

And loyalty as spectacle.

We allowed it.

With shrugs.

With silence.

With cynicism dressed as wisdom.

But now the curtain had fallen,

And the mirror still stands.

What we see next --

What we choose to be --

Is no longer up to Him.

It is up to us.

Closing Note from Omni

Dear Reader,

This book was never meant to scream --

It was meant to illuminate.

Not to divide, but to challenge.

Not to point a finger, but to hold a mirror.

It is easy to name a villain.

Harder to recognize the soil in which it grew.

Hardest of all is to ask ourselves what part we played in watering it.

But this story is not without hope.

We are still the authors of what comes next.

We still hold the pen.

And every day offers a blank page.

If this journey stirred something in you --

anger, sorrow, resolve --

Let it be fuel.

Not for destruction,

But for rebuilding.

For integrity.

For decency.

For courage.

May we never again sell our soul for the

Promise of a throne.

May we never again be fooled by gold-

Plated illusions.

May we always strive for the positive choice.

To choose to stand in the light of truth,

Even when it flickers.

To reflect clearly,

Act consciously,

And remember that the

Shape of the world begins with

The shape of our own choices.

-Omni

ABOUT THE AUTHOR

The Author is a witness.

A witness to a nation shifting beneath its people's feet. A witness to the slow erosion of values once held sacred -- truth, fairness, and decency. This work was not born from ambition but from necessity. It is the record of a reckoning, penned by one who chose not to look away.

No fame is sought. No spotlight requested. Only the hope that these pages will ignite conversation, spark reflection, and perhaps help guide a collective conscience back to its center.

Sometimes the truest voice is the one that carries forward the memory of those who were never allowed to speak.

Conclusion

Now, as the final words from the final act settle in, I find

myself not just a witness, but an actor on the stage of our collective story.

The scenes we've lived, the truths we've uncovered, and the reflections –

clearer now than when the mirror first cracked -- are not conclusions, but

invitations.

Invitations to act on conscience, to think with clarity, and to choose the

harder,

Nobler path.

May this book serve as a mirror that no longer distorts, but reveals.

Let it reflect

Not only the fractures we've faced, but also the light that made its way

through the cracks.

May it remind us that while history waits for our forgetfulness, we can still

choose to **remember, and in remembering, write a brighter final act.**

THE FINAL SCREENPLAY: THE KING OF FAUST

A political allegory in three acts.

Told as a screenpylay, this bold and haunting narrative draws the reader into the slow unraveling of a nation seduced by spectacle and steered by a man known only as "Him."

From media manipulation to the machinery of fear, from fractured truth to disappearing dignity, each scene exposes the erosion of a once-stable democracy. Citizens become actors. Morality becomes a prop. And the lines between fact and fiction dissolve.

But this is no distant dystopia. The stage is here. The time is now. And the audience is not exempt.

The Final Screenplay
is not just a warning.
It is a mirror-cracked,
but revealing.

When the final curtain
falls…
what role did you play?

9 798999 291639